MW00423539

Bold faith stands on the shoulders of quiet trust. Chris Overstreet has faithfully developed this kind of trust in the Lord, and he is now one of the boldest preachers of the Gospel I know. In his new book, *Faith That Sees*, Chris shares from his own story and strengthens the call for all believers to experience the fruit of a faith-filled life. Chris is a great inspiration to the Church, encouraging us to live from the unseen, walk in the promises of God, and allow heaven's perspective to become our own.

Bill Johnson • Bethel Church, Redding, CA
Author of *The Way of Life* and
Raising Giant-Killers

Faith is the catalyst to the impossible, the prognosis of the probable, and the potential in the powerful. When circumstances are dire and people become downcast, faith pounds a pillar of possibility into the hearts of the hopeless. Furthermore, Jesus is the great Author of our faith; He knows how to wield words that will mobilize you into your destiny and shape chapters of your life to bring you into the fullness of who He created you to be!

In *Faith That Sees* by Chris Overstreet, you will gain practical insights to grow your faith by stewarding what God has already placed in your hands. I highly recommend this book to anyone who is hungry to know the heart of the Father in a deeper way, to gain unshakeable confidence in their destiny, and take risks to step out in greater faith. Open these pages with an expectant heart, ready to be launched into a lifestyle where the impossible is now supernaturally possible through Christ!

Kris Vallotton • Leader, Bethel Church, Redding, CA •
Co-Founder of Bethel School of Supernatural Ministry
Author of twelve books, including *The Supernatural Ways of Royalty*, *Heavy Rain*, and *Poverty, Riches and Wealth*

Chris Overstreet not only loves to share the Gospel, but he also loves to equip others to share the Good News of our Savior. In *Faith That Sees*, Chris shares powerful tools for growing our faith and evangelistic effectiveness through personally encountering His Word and His love. The testimonies he shares will inspire you greatly to proclaim the Gospel like never before. Thank you, Chris, for your relentless pursuit to know Jesus and make Him known.

Steve Backlund • Founder, Igniting Hope Ministries

From the moment I met Chris I knew I was meeting someone on fire for Jesus and for proclaiming the Good News. Few people are so filled with faith and love that they're willing to share the Gospel on a daily basis. Whether he's sharing with large crowds, door to door, or on the streets of Portland, Chris models a faith that sees people's needs and sees them in the way God sees them; as people in need of His love and care. Chris has a unique way of inspiring everyday believers to believe God can use them.

Kevin Palau • President and CEO, Luis Palau Association

Chris Overstreet shares on how to see from heaven's perspective. Chris's authenticity, passion and heart to share the Gospel is contagious. This book may be that mustard seed that produces the type of faith that moves a mountain.

Chuck McCallum • Catalyst Business School Founder and Businessman

As a Jesus follower I've found a consistent need to have people in my life I can listen to, whose voice echoes God's voice. The journey of life we're all in the midst of requires guides and examples that help us stay close to Jesus and His intentions for us. I've found Chris to be one of those voices. His heart and his life are a rare example to me of one laid down for Jesus, who is in full pursuit of the purity of heaven. Chris has always been an example to me of Jesus in skin. This book will feel like a taste of heaven. It will challenge you and encourage you to live into and toward those things God has invited you into. "Follow me", Jesus said, "I will make you fishers of men." Chris speaks in the same spirit and with the same kind of God-given (his Father's) authority. You'll be marked. Read and be refreshed.

Lance Jacobs • Associate Leader and City Team Director, Bethel Redding

Faith That Sees is not a book, it's a voice of empowerment! Chris articulates the profound truths that release us from the slumber of passivity and stir us to live out the divine destiny we were all called to live. Through powerful stories and biblical insights, Chris will help you realize that partnering with the Holy Spirit will lead you on a destiny adventure!

Mike Tatlock • Lead Pastor, Grace Chapel Wilsonville

Chris burns like few people I have ever met. His commitment to Christ, and passion to see America saved is real. His love for God and people is a gift to the world, but behind this mighty evangelist is a powerful story of someone who has gone from tragedy to triumph. He is an overcomer whose story has impacted thousands, and shaped him to be a man who sees through heaven's possibilities. His faith will encourage, equip, and propel you into a life with power and love. Get ready to be encouraged!

Tom Crandell • Director of Young Saints
Bethel Church, Redding CA

ISBN: 9781689639484
Cover design by Ricky Russ Jr • www.ricky.news
For Worldwide Distribution, Printed in the USA.

FAITH THAT SEES

By Chris Overstreet

To my beautiful wife, Stefanie, and your desire to step out in faith as you start a business that will help women with postpartum depression.

Your breakthrough, honey, is now going to help thousands of other women.

Table of Contents

Introduction

I met a woman named Janie who spent twelve years of her life in a wheelchair due to a rare disease. At a Christian music festival, some of our Compassion To Action team felt led to ask if they could pray for her and being nice and polite, she did not want to refuse. The team felt very strongly that God wanted to heal her. At first, Janie did not feel anything, but as they continued to pray, she began to feel something change.

Janie had struggled with depression most of her life and wanted to believe that one day she would walk again, but she wasn't sure she had enough faith left. One of the team members asked if she would take a step of faith. Scared but hopeful she stood to her feet, and suddenly she felt God's presence on her legs. As Janie began to walk, she felt as though she were wearing supernatural leg braces, and even though her muscles were atrophied and she wobbled a little bit, with each step the power of God strengthened her legs. He was healing her. She was overcome with the power of Jesus' love for her and amazed that He would heal her.[1]

Like Janie, you may also feel that even though you have faith, your faith has atrophied because you

---

1 To hear Janie's story, please visit our website at compassiontoaction.com/janies-testimony

have not used it much. I encourage you today that you will see your faith grow by stepping out in what God has already given you.

At the start of every new year, many people reflect on their goals from the previous year and begin to set new goals for the year ahead. The sad news is that studies reveal that most people give up after the first week of setting goals. They lose faith in the goal because their current reality looks different. They fail to focus on the vision and what is unseen, and instead grow discouraged by what they can see in the tangible world.

What would happen if we allowed faith to lead us to action? The gold Miners in the famous California Gold Rush were said to have extracted more than 750,000 pounds of gold, but it began with the discovery of a single gold nugget. Gold was first discovered in California in 1848, but the gold rush reached a height of frenzy in 1849 when people developed gold fever and flooded California in hopes of striking it rich. Why then? Was the gold always there or did it happen to appear because of the way the earth moved? I think it was always there and once the miners discovered the gold, people's faith came alive because they believed they were going to find some as well.

I wonder if there was anyone else who could have discovered the gold prior to 1848, but who gave up too soon. Faith works in much the same way. Often, faith is not what we can see in the natural but what we sense in the unseen world that keeps us digging until we hit the target, until we strike gold.

Faith is required for our future and vital in our development to fulfill who God has called us to be and what He has called us to do. As you read through *Faith That Sees*, make a commitment to yourself that you will not settle for anything less than what God has created you to be and do in this life. Faith in Jesus Christ will help you to discover the value that you have and the future that is worth pursuing. Be bold and courageous like Joshua and Caleb, who knew that the Israelites could conquer the land that God had promised them. They challenged the people to move forward into God's promise. Instead of sitting back quietly and backing down in fear, they saw from the perspective of another realm that says it is possible; we will take the land!

ONE
TWO
THREE
FOUR
FIVE
SIX
SEVEN
EIGHT
NINE

1

Seeing Through Faith

> If you can't fly then run, if you can't run
> then walk, if you can't walk then crawl, but
> whatever you do, you have to keep moving
> forward.

–Martin Luther King Jr., Cleveland, Ohio 1967

How did I get this big? I thought. I had already lost
some weight, down from my original four hundred
pounds, but I knew I needed more in life than just
trying to lose weight. I struggled with feelings of
failure most of my childhood and while I earnestly
sought to achieve a vision for my life for years, it
wasn't until I began to see myself the way God sees
me that things began to change. I needed to learn
how to see my life through faith.

It was during this journey that I received a prophetic word from a man who was a guest speaker
at a church I attended. "Stop being hard on yourself
when you look in the mirror!" he said. "There is a
great man of God inside of you, and He wants you
to see it. Do you know God gets angry? He doesn't
like it when you give yourself a hard time because
when you do, you're giving Him a hard time as well
and he doesn't want you to do that anymore." He
went on to say, "You know what rejection feels like,

and God is telling you to go to those who feel rejected." How did this man, who did not know me, know that I spent hours throughout the day giving myself a hard time? How did he know that I felt rejected most of my childhood and teenage years and like I never fit in?

The word of the Lord came to me at that moment. He wanted to feed me real food, food that would change my soul from hellish thinking. God saved my spirit and yet, my mind needed major transformation. I needed to see myself the way He sees me. Not long after hearing that prophetic word, I remember the Lord telling me to stand in front of the mirror. As I stood there in front of the mirror, I could feel God speaking to my heart. He told me to speak out loud in faith what God the Father thinks of me and how my life was going to change for the better: "For as he thinks in his heart, so is he" (Proverbs 23:7). In faith, I obeyed. I did not want to give God a hard time anymore by giving myself a hard time. If I were to continue thinking and speaking negatively over my life, I would be sinning against God because I knew what He had asked me to do.

When I began speaking affirmations over myself, it felt fake and very uncomfortable like I was making it up. Over the years my mind had developed strongholds of self-hatred that constantly told me I was a failure. I still felt the effects of belittling myself even though God had recently forgiven me of all my sin. He reprogrammed my mind through the discipline of writing down scriptures that affirmed who I am in Him. I started to discover what God truly thought about me. These declarations enabled me to overcome the lies I had believed for so long.

A New Language

Our words are powerful! They speak life or death. They can create either an atmosphere of fear and death or faith and life. That is why the affirmations and declarations I spoke over myself were so life changing. Understanding that God spoke the world into existence impacts the words we choose.

> By the word of the LORD the heavens were made, and all the host of them by the breath of His mouth. He gathers the waters of the sea together as a heap; He lays up the deep in storehouses. Let all the earth fear the LORD; Let all the inhabitants of the world stand in awe of Him. For He spoke, and it was *done*; He commanded, and it stood fast.
>
> Psalm 33:6-9

Words and thoughts combined have power. According to scientific research by a leading scientist and born-again Christian, Dr. Caroline Leaf, what we think and speak affects us physically and emotionally. She reveals the transformational power of knowing and meditating on God's Word in her book, *Who Switched Off My Brain?* During my journey of faith, I discovered that I desperately needed a new vocabulary and a new language. Through faith and patience, a new language formed on my lips. I stood in front of the mirror and said out loud, "Chris Overstreet, look at me. You're a man of God, and God's hand is on your life. God is for you, and there

7

is something great about your life. You are not a failure!" As I read and recited the Word of God the strongholds and fortresses around my mind slowly began to crumble, and a vision of who I am began to surface.

Faith Leads to Transformation

I saw a glimpse of the new, real me; spirit, soul, and body. I became a healthier person filled with God's Word by faith, and I had also lost weight! I no longer lived with the fear of rejection. Instead, I felt compassion for others who had been rejected and wanted to help them. Peace began to form roots in my life, "You will keep *him* in perfect peace, *whose* mind *is* stayed *on You,* because he trusts in You" (Isaiah 26:3). I felt God's peace come over me when I began to trust Him. The peace of God helps build a long-lasting Godly vision for your life.

The word *mind* in this passage from Isaiah means "creative imaginations." The peace of God supports the creative imagination. For the first time in my life, I began to see what it looked and felt like to be the person God created me to be.

As I began to pray in the Holy Spirit, and read and declare God's Word in faith, my spirit began to dream. I would close my eyes and envision myself changing from a caterpillar as it transforms into a butterfly, and throughout the day I would thank God for His grace and power to change. It felt like I was watching the God-vision movie of my life unfold. I was changing because my belief system and thought processes began to change.

The grace of God is the power of God to cause personal metamorphosis. The Apostle Paul reminds us, "Do not be conformed to this world, but be transformed by the renewing of your mind, that you may prove what *is* that good and acceptable and perfect will of God" (Romans 12:2). I turned my back on old thinking. I wanted to demolish every thought process that had brought me pain and led to destructive habits that sabotaged my future. Renewal of my mind enabled me to step into the good and acceptable and perfect will of God for my life. Faith began to surface in my heart; it came alive. I became convinced of what I saw in my heart. What felt fake and uncomfortable at one time became normal practice in my life. In faith, I received God's vision and transformation through the power of His Word.

When you see yourself the way God sees you, you are looking at yourself through eyes of love and humility. Your life is significant and important. You may think that self-criticism does God a favor by helping you stay humble, but the opposite is true. He looks for humility and a surrendered heart. Your life is like a book, and in every chapter of that book, God is looking at your heart. As you write your book, my prayer is that you would see yourself the way that God sees you and that faith would come alive in your heart so that you will be the man or woman He has called you to be.

ONE

TWO

THREE

FOUR

FIVE

SIX

SEVEN

EIGHT

NINE

2
My Whole Hand

Never be afraid to trust an unknown future
to a known God.

–Corrie ten Boom

In January 2000, I stood worshiping Jesus with
some young missionaries in Tepic, Mexico, and as
I did, I started to hear God speak to me in a vision.
It was so clear and vivid; it felt as if I viewed it on
a movie screen. I saw the hand of the Lord Jesus
stretched out toward me from heaven, and He said,
Trust me. Then He said to take hold of His whole
hand to see what He would do with my life. *Do not
take hold of just one finger, two fingers, three fingers, four fingers, but with your whole hand take
hold of my hand and trust me and watch what I will
do in and through your life.*

As I reached out in the vision to take hold of His
hand, suddenly I saw a tornado come close to me,
and as soon as it drew near, I was swallowed up in
the wind. The Spirit of the Lord said, *I am going to
do a work inside of you that you never thought would
take place and I am going to take you places that you
never thought you would go, as long as you trust me.*
While He spoke these precious words of life to my
spirit, faith came alive inside of me. I realized that if

I trusted Him with everything, the Holy Spirit would be the operative Person of power in my life.

Acknowledging God

Trusting God requires faith to believe He is who He says He is and will do what He says He will do. To trust God is to surrender and give up control as we acknowledge that God is the one who governs our lives. "In all your ways acknowledge Him, and He shall direct your paths" (Proverbs 3:6). There are two important words in Proverbs 3:6: the word *acknowledge* and the word *direct*. In Hebrew, the word *acknowledge* is *Yada*. When translated it means "to know," meaning to know by observation, investigation, reflection or firsthand experience. But the highest level of *Yada* is in direct, intimate contact. It refers to life-giving intimacy, as in a marriage with a husband and wife.

In a spiritual context, it suggests an intimate relationship between God and prayer. It is the highest heart-to-heart connection between man and God. This type of intimacy with God through prayer births blessings and victories. I want God to bless me, and I want God to bless you, and one of the ways He does that is by directing our steps.

The word *direct* in the Hebrew is *Yashar,* and it means to "make straight" or "make right." God will straighten the path of those who are devoted to Him and who will trust and acknowledge Him in all their ways. Imagine walking on a crooked path that has a cliff on either side. When we trust God, He will clear the way, lead us safely, and right the crooked paths. God said, "I will go before you and make the crooked places straight; I will break in pieces the gates of bronze and cut the bars of iron" (Isaiah 45:2). God wants to help direct our steps.

There have been many times throughout my life when I did not know what to do. I would return to the Word of God to remind myself how much I can trust Him. Trust is not always a feeling but a commitment of faith that comes from the heart. When I interact with young people who have the vision to do something great for God, they say something like this, "Chris I have a passion and vision to reach thousands of people with the Gospel, but I don't know where to start." The desire to reach thousands of people for Jesus Christ is a great and noble vision. How you go about it may look different for each one of you. The foundational truth is that you must believe in the One who gives the vision more than you believe the vision itself.

Your faith and trust in God prepare a steadfast heart that seeks His kingdom first and foremost. Jesus said to "Seek first the kingdom of God and His righteousness, and all these things shall be added to you" (Matthew 6:33). Your faith is lit on fire to seek and pray into the vision God has given you when you trust Him for being who He is. Based on this secure foundation, you are free to dream and anticipate the vision in your heart and mind. Once trust and faith are active in your heart, action will follow.

Envisioning Truth

Often in my early twenties, I would pace back and forth in the early morning praying to receive the heart of God. I wanted to follow Him at any cost and do whatever He told me to do. Faith rose inside of me that I would preach the Gospel as I meditated on these words.

> Later He appeared to the eleven as they sat at the table; and He rebuked their unbelief and hardness of heart, because they did not believe those who had seen Him after He had risen. And He said to them, "Go into all the world and preach the gospel to every creature. He who believes and is baptized will be saved; but he who does not believe will be condemned. And these signs will follow those who believe: In My name, they will cast out demons; they will speak with new tongues; they will take up serpents; and if they drink anything deadly, it will by no means hurt them; they will lay hands on the sick, and they will recover." So then, after the Lord had spoken to them, He was received up into heaven, and sat down at the right hand of God. And they went out and preached everywhere, the Lord working with *them* and confirming the word through the accompanying signs. Amen.

Mark 16:14-20

I wrote this scripture on a three-by-five card and carried it with me to work. I would pull that card out and read it repeatedly. I am a believer, and the Bible says these signs shall follow my life. I will lay my hands on the sick, and they will recover. I began to confess this truth. I would come home after work and open my Bible and study the Word of God. I believed I could do what it said I could do. I would act it out as if I was on the streets and imagine approaching a man who had pain in his legs and knees. Then I would imagine laying my hands on his knee and commanding all the pain to leave. *How does it feel?* I would say.

In response, I would imagine him saying that all the pain was gone. *That is amazing! Praise God!* I would also imagine myself preaching about Jesus Christ and His death and resurrection. It was as though I was watching a sneak preview at a spiritual movie theater. As I began to pray, my heart would see through the eyes of faith. I would rejoice when I saw myself praying with someone who I imagined had just repented of their sins, received salvation, and decided to follow Jesus Christ.

God was preparing me to see in my imagination what He declared I could and would do as a believer. Through prayer I was able to create with Jesus. I felt the "perfect peace" of God take root in my heart as I continued to meditate on this truth in Isaiah (Isaiah 26:3). The word *peace* in Hebrew is *shalom*, and it defines what true peace is and how peace has the power to calm any storm in your mind. As I shared previously, the word *mind* in this passage means "creative imagination." So, when you set your mind on God and His truth, His peace guards your heart and mind, and you, too, will create with Jesus.

My heart began to see, through heaven's perspective, what God has for me and how it would require faith in action to put it into practice. He began to speak to me about telling my neighbors about Jesus. So, when I was twenty-one, I imagined walking around my neighborhood telling my neighbors how much Jesus loves them and asking if they needed prayer for anything.

After envisioning it, I took a step of faith and walked door-to-door. I was amazed at the receptivity and how many people wanted me to pray for them. Following Jesus became an adventure, not a burden, but a true joy of my heart!

Following Jesus

And as He walked by the Sea of Galilee, He saw Simon and Andrew his brother casting a net into the sea; for they were fishermen. Then Jesus said to them, "Follow Me, and I will make you become fishers of men." They immediately left their nets and followed Him. When He had gone a little farther from there, He saw James the son of Zebedee, and

John his brother, who also were in the boat mending their nets. And immediately He called them, and they left their father Zebedee in the boat with the hired servants, and went after Him.

Mark 1:16-20

When Jesus called the four young fishermen Simon, Andrew, James, and John to follow Him, He did not tell them where He was going. To leave the family fishing business required complete trust from these young men! Jesus said to follow Him, and He would make them fishers of men. These words probably did not make much logical sense to them, but something profoundly powerful must have impacted their hearts for them to leave the family business to follow someone whom they did not know. The words that Jesus spoke are always full of life, and although they had no clue where Jesus was going, His words fed the inner longing of their hearts. Following Jesus is an adventure and these young fishermen chose to embark on a hands-on, lifelong mission trip with Jesus, the One who holds the world in His hands.

Jesus broke all of the legalistic rules of the day. The disciples discovered that not everyone liked Jesus and they had to make an ongoing choice to follow and obey Him. It is important to take note that following Jesus in faith is not like joining a Christian country club. Following Him requires a commitment and a heart that anchors itself in the love and obedience of God. Empowered by faith, and through God's grace, the heart knows that Jesus

is the only way. After these young ones started following Jesus, they went to Capernaum and immediately, on the Sabbath, He entered the synagogue
and taught. Jesus' teaching was very different from
the teachings of the religious leaders of the day because He spoke with spiritual authority. Speaking
with spiritual authority is a good lesson for us to
learn. True spiritual authority can be felt from, and
seen, on a person who is sent by God.

Imagine the first day of the disciples' mission trip as
they watched Jesus teach. Everyone was captivated
by His atmospheric, spiritual authority. Suddenly,
a man with a demon interrupted His teaching. Demons always try to disturb a move of God. I wonder
how the disciples felt. They had just started to follow Jesus. Was the hair on their arms standing up?
Jesus commanded the demon to be silent and come
out of the man. Suddenly, the demonized man cried
out, and the demon came out of him. Everyone was
amazed at the authority with which Jesus taught. He
stood out. The truth is that when you have the faith
to walk in the power of the Spirit, you will stand out
in spiritual authority too!

The young disciples chose to go on the adventure
of a lifetime with Jesus that would lead them on a
path of no return and no plan B! But first, their faith
needed to be strengthened to endure the hardships
that they would face along the way.

Today, there is a generation on the rise that is hungry, not to go to church, but to *be* the Church and
to follow Jesus at any cost. As you read through the
rest of this book, I declare that faith will arise in

your heart to believe that YOU were born for such a time as this. Believe it and receive it in your spirit. It will affect the course of your life.

ONE

TWO

THREE

FOUR

FIVE

SIX

SEVEN

EIGHT

NINE

3

The Author of Faith

Looking unto Jesus, the author and finisher of *our* faith, who for the joy that was set before Him endured the cross, despising the shame, and has sat down at the right hand of the throne of God.

–Hebrews 12:2

As a new Christian, there were many times I faced discouragement because I compared myself to the Christians I read about and those around me. As I read about the great heroes of the faith and how their lives shaped the course of history, my heart ignited with a fire and a passion for Jesus.

At the same time, I felt like my life could never measure up to the lives of these men and women who were so greatly used by God. I would think, *how can I grow faster in faith? If I need to fast three days a week, I will! No matter the cost, I want to pay it.* I loved Jesus with all my heart and wanted to grow as a new disciple. I saw how others seemed to be much further along than I was, which made me feel like I was still wearing "spiritual" diapers.

Eventually, though, I discovered that Jesus was writing my faith story, not me. With this realization, a huge weight came off my chest. I was freed to believe that God predestined my story. He was the One who dreamed me up in His heart and planned my life; He planned my entire existence. God is doing for you just as He did for Jeremiah, "For I know the thoughts that I think toward you, says the LORD, thoughts of peace and not of evil, to give you a future and a hope" (Jeremiah 29:11). Your life is a book. Let Jesus Christ write the manuscript!

Seeing from Heaven's Perspective

Your book has many chapters. In each chapter, you can live in faith instead of fear and regret. Growing as a disciple and walking in faith has to do with trusting the author and finisher of your story. I used to feel insecure that the chapter of my book was not as fiery, fruitful or miraculous as I thought it should be. But growing in faith does not come by striving or trying harder. It comes by abiding in the faithful One. The more you look at Him and spend time with Him the more you look like Him. Jesus Christ is the source of faith and the author of your life. When you spend time with Him, strength comes into your spirit-man and the eyes of your heart are opened to see as He sees.

Consider this story from the Book of John:

> After these things Jesus went over the Sea of Galilee, which is *the Sea* of Tiberias. Then a great multitude followed Him, because they saw His signs which He performed on those

who were diseased. And Jesus went up on the mountain, and there He sat with His disciples. Now the Passover, a feast of the Jews, was near. Then Jesus lifted up *His* eyes, and seeing a great multitude coming toward Him, He said to Philip, "Where shall we buy bread, that these may eat?" But this He said to test him, for He Himself knew what He would do. Philip answered Him, "Two hundred denarii worth of bread is not sufficient for them, that every one of them may have a little." One of His disciples, Andrew, Simon Peter's brother, said to Him, "There is a lad here who has five barley loaves and two small fish, but what are they among so many?" Then Jesus said, "Make the people sit down." Now there was much grass in the place. So the men sat down, in number about five thousand. And Jesus took the loaves, and when He had given thanks He distributed *them* to the disciples, and the disciples to those sitting down; and likewise of the fish, as much as they wanted. So when they were filled, He said to His disciples, "Gather up the fragments that remain, so that nothing is lost." Therefore they gathered *them* up, and filled twelve baskets with the fragments of the five barley loaves which were left over by those who had eaten.

John 6:1-13

When Jesus saw that the multitudes were hungry and weary, He saw from heaven's perspective. Heaven's perspective comes from the heart of the Father, which is the heart of compassion. Jesus' eyes of compassion led Him to take an act of faith. His compassion led to action. From heaven's perspective, Jesus functioned not only from compassion but also from abundance. Jesus didn't just feed everyone there; He even planned for everyone to have enough for leftovers!

The disciples only saw a few loaves and fish in the natural realm, which limited their ability to see what the Father was doing. They wondered how Jesus had fed so many. At that moment, the disciples only saw in one dimension, which prevented them from seeing Who had been standing right next to them for three years! They did not see that they had full access to God Himself through the Person of Jesus and that in Him all things were possible.

Faith sees from heaven's perspective. Like Jesus, when we look with the eyes of faith, we will see from the perspective of compassion, abundance, hope, and expectancy. Seeing from this perspective will lead us to step out and act in boldness, expecting God to do the impossible.

Hearing God

No matter what season you are in, understand that the author of faith, Jesus Christ, is with you. Faith comes by hearing His Word spoken in your heart.

By His grace and power, the life in the Word of God causes growth as faith takes root in your heart. "So, then faith *comes* by hearing, and hearing by the word of God" (Romans 10:17).

In the context of that passage, God celebrates the act of faith as the preacher, or the proclaimer takes steps of faith and preaches the message of saving and empowering grace. Hearing the Word of God does not have to be a complicated issue once we purpose in our hearts that He is the Shepherd and we are His sheep, and His sheep hear His voice (John 10:27). We are His children by a spiritual birth. When one is born again, the Holy Spirit—the Spirit of Truth— reveals the truth to our spirit-man. The awakening of the heart is a miracle; it is the greatest miracle. Faith comes alive in the heart when an individual hears God speak to him or her.

Often, when I read the Bible, I wait to see what jumps off the page to stir my heart and faith. There have been many times when I read the Word of God out loud, and upon hearing it, I received a deeper deposit of faith in my spirit. I believe it is important for us to approach the Word of God with the expectation to hear from Him. The Bible holds hundreds of promises for God's children who believe. The author of our life has given us the ability to search out what He has already said about us.

After becoming born again, my spirit-man was free, but my mind needed major transformation, and I knew that getting to know the One who saved me would help bring truth to my mind and thinking. Through my love for Jesus and God's Word, I began to develop a listening relationship with Jesus. It did not happen through a step-by-step ritual but through my hunger for a deeper relationship with Him. I remember receiving a word from God that came differently than usual.

I learned how to spend time with the Lord reading my Bible and asking what was on His heart. I would then share what was on my heart as an exchange. This time, however, He spoke to me through a few individuals who were guest speakers when I attended Youth With A Mission, YWAM. One of those speakers was Kris Vallotton, a pastor from Bethel Church in Redding, California. I did not know him at the time, although he would eventually become my mentor and overseer. He gave me a prophetic word that rapidly changed my perspective on my life and future.

I could feel God's presence all around me as Kris and the student team that traveled with him began to prophecy over me, and as the prophetic word took root in my spirit. His prophetic word began with Romans 1:16-17, "For I am not ashamed of the gospel of Christ, for it is the power of God to salvation for everyone who believes, for the Jew first and also for the Greek. For in it the righteousness of God is revealed from faith to faith; as it is written, 'The just shall live by faith.'"

Kris said, "I see that God is making you bold, and He is taking away your shame." He explained to me that one of David's mighty men in the Bible, Eleazar, had battled long and hard with the enemy when his hand became tired and froze to his sword. He did not let go. Kris prophesied that, like Eleazar, I would take hold of God's word over my life and not let go. Then he quoted from Hebrews 4:12, "For the Word of God *is* living and powerful." He asked me if I had heard of Carlos Annacondia who wrote the book, *Listen to Me, Satan!* And then he said that I, too, am a pure evangelist and would have a ministry like Carlos Annacondia's, with miracles, signs, and wonders following my life. I felt the power of God released and revealed in a new way over my life as Kris declared these words. I felt God's heart for the lost more deeply than I ever had before. I meditated on this prophetic word day and night.

The Bible, in 1 Corinthians 12:4-11, teaches us about the importance of the gifts of the Spirit for the profit of all, and prophecy is one of those gifts. Knowing its importance, I felt the responsibility to steward that prophetic word through faith. I felt life stir inside of my heart as Kris proclaimed that word. I realized that if I did not continually value what God said, that I was quenching the Spirit of God in my life. And, 1 Thessalonians 5:19-22 warns us, "Do not quench the Spirit. Do not despise prophecies. Test all things; hold fast what is good. Abstain from every form of evil." I am commanded not to quench the Spirit and not to despise prophecies, but that I should test them holding onto that which is good!

Walking in Faith

My faith began to rise as my spirit received the

word about boldly sharing the Gospel. The prophetic word began to take on legs for the direction of my life. I had already been sharing my faith out of pure obedience to God's Word. I was a believer, and as I studied God's Word and asked for His heart, He showed me that people *are* His heart. As I continued listening to this prophetic word, I knew that God was calling me into the ministry. Lies fell away as faith came alive in me. I began to see more clearly from God's view rather than my own.

As I listened intentionally, the word *evangelist* kept coming up. I was called to be an evangelist, and miracles, signs, and wonders would follow my life and confirm the word I was preaching. Faith surfaced in my heart that helped dispel lies that I believed concerning my future. I held onto that word and meditated on it day and night. I wanted to progress in God's calling. I made a choice not to neglect this prophecy but to meditate on these things and to give myself entirely to it. I felt like young Timothy when he received a prophetic word from Paul.

> Do not neglect the gift that is in you, which was given to you by prophecy with the laying on of the hands of the eldership. Meditate on these things; give yourself entirely to them, that your progress may be evident to all. Take heed to yourself and to the doctrine. Continue in them, for in doing this you will save both yourself and those who hear you.
>
> 1 Timothy 4:14-16

I believed God's word for my life and knew that I had a responsibility to participate in that word. I needed to walk out the word through faith and look for the opportunities that God put in front of me. I began to pray, *God, what can I do? How can I be more effective in sharing my faith?*

The Lord began to show me that many young people go to the mall to hang out and that it was a great opportunity to share the Gospel with them and to see them saved. I honestly did not know what I was doing but I had a passion, and I depended on the Holy Spirit to lead and guide me. Every Friday I would go to the mall to share the Gospel. I was amazed at the number of teenagers who would get saved as I shared the simple Gospel of Jesus Christ. I always looked for a large group that I could approach.

As I approached, I would introduce myself and begin to ask them a series of questions. *By chance, has anyone ever told you what it means to be born again?* I would wait to see what they would say. Most of them would say no. *Do you mind if I tell you what it means?* When they responded that they were willing to listen, I opened my small Bible and turned to the gospel of John.

> There was a man of the Pharisees named Nicodemus, a ruler of the Jews. This man came to Jesus by night and said to Him, "Rabbi, we know that You are a teacher come from God; for no one can do these signs that You do unless God is with him." Jesus answered and said to him, "Most assuredly, I say to you, unless one is born again, he cannot see

the kingdom of God." Nicodemus said to Him, "How can a man be born when he is old? Can he enter a second time into his mother's womb and be born?" Jesus answered, "Most assuredly, I say to you, unless one is born of water and the Spirit, he cannot enter the kingdom of God. That which is born of the flesh is flesh, and that which is born of the Spirit is spirit. Do not marvel that I said to you, 'You must be born again.' The wind blows where it wishes, and you hear the sound of it, but cannot tell where it comes from and where it goes. So is everyone who is born of the Spirit." Nicodemus answered and said to Him, "How can these things be?" Jesus answered and said to him, "Are you the teacher of Israel, and do not know these things? Most assuredly, I say to you, We speak what We know and testify what We have seen, and you do not receive Our witness. If I have told you earthly things and you do not believe, how will you believe if I tell you heavenly things? No one has ascended to heaven but He who came down from heaven, *that is*, the Son of Man who is in heaven. And as Moses lifted up the serpent in the wilderness, even so must the Son of Man be lifted up, that whoever believes in Him should not perish but have eternal life. For God so loved the world that He gave His only begotten Son, that whoever believes in Him should not perish but have everlasting life. For God did not send His Son into the world to condemn the world, but that the world through Him might be saved."

John 3:1-17

I would go on to explain that while we are all born physically from our mothers, there is another birth, a spiritual birth through which we are born of the Spirit. I would tell them that Jesus is the son of God and that He loves them. *Do you believe that Jesus Christ died on the cross for you?* Many would say yes. *Do you believe that He rose again?* Again, some would say yes. *Did you know that you could become a child of God if you receive Him?* I would share that the Bible says in John 1:12 that, "As many as received Him, to them He gave the right to become children of God, to those who believe in His name."

Then I would ask another question. *Do you believe that He can save you and forgive you of your sins?* Many of them would say yes. I got so excited as I began to share from Romans 10:9, that "If you confess with your mouth the Lord Jesus and believe in your heart that God has raised Him from the dead, you will be saved." I would ask a final question. *Do you believe with all your heart?* When they answered yes, I would pray with them right then to give their lives to Jesus and receive forgiveness of sins.

Many people in that mall received Christ Jesus, and every time I shared my faith it was imparted into their hearts, and my faith got stronger and stronger. I meditated day and night on the word of God over my life. Looking back, I would do some things differently, such as getting these new disciples plugged into a community of believers, but you only do what you know at the time.

After faithfully sharing the Gospel week in and week out, seeking God's direction, and knowing that Jesus is the author and finisher of my faith, I felt like something was about to change in my life. God, the author of faith, was guiding my steps, writing the next chapter of my story, and was in complete control as I submitted to Him. John 15:4 reminds us that the branch cannot bear fruit unless it abides in the vine and we cannot bear fruit unless we abide in Jesus. When you are committed and submitted to Him, His plan comes to fruition. His plan was about to come to fruition in my life. I had no idea that what was about to take place would change the course of my life forever.

ONE
TWO
THREE
FOUR
FIVE
SIX
SEVEN
EIGHT
NINE

4
Follow the Leader

If God is your partner, make your plans
BIG!

–D.L. Moody

I felt a stirring in my heart to pray and fast for the
direction that God had for my life. I knew that He
was working on my heart regarding the tangible ex-
pression of ministry. I felt the call of God, but I was
not sure what that fully entailed or how it would
look. I just knew that I was called to seek Him with
all my heart and to acknowledge Him.

Obeying His Voice

Trusting that God was leading me, I started waiting
tables. Serving people in a restaurant was a practical illustration of what God was doing in my heart. I
wanted to learn how to serve God and people. Jesus
came to serve others, not to be served. I knew that I
needed His heart.

One night, while I was sleeping, I was awakened
by the voice of God speaking to me audibly. I had
heard stories of God speaking to people in dreams
and even read in the Bible about how God spoke to

Samuel when he was a child in 1 Samuel chapter 3. Hearing His audible voice was new for me and shook me at my core.

The voice of the Lord shouted at me, saying, *YOU WILL BE MOVING! Moving?,* I thought. At that time, I was living in St. Louis, Missouri waiting tables in my hometown where I grew up.

For the next month and a half, while working, I thought about the strange encounter I had that night. I thought about how the Lord spoke this directional word to me about moving. I wondered, *Where am I moving to, Lord? You spoke to me, but you never told me where I am going.* I prayed to Him; *I'll go anywhere You want me to go. Lord, I want to do what You want me to do.*

After a month and a half of praying and seeking God's will for my life, I heard Him speak clearly to my heart saying that I was to move to Redding, California to attend the Bethel Church School of Supernatural Ministry where I would be trained and equipped for what He was calling me to do in the future. I knew I had heard from God, and I was so excited to tell my family.

As I began to share with others about the direction in which God was leading me, some people outside of my family told me that I had missed it; I was not hearing God and I should not move. Some of the people that shared this with me were dear friends that I loved very much. I knew that when they shared their thoughts with me, it was just their opinion, and everyone has an opinion. It was a test for me to determine whether to believe God or to believe what other people think I should be doing with my life.

Praise God that I listened to Him because I am seeing the fruit of trusting and obeying Him even as I write this book. I was so excited to hear God speak and have Him lead and guide my life. It is exciting to know that God has much bigger plans for our lives than we do.

Although many people tried to talk me out of moving—some told me to remain where I was so I could be a youth pastor—I knew that if I stayed, I would not be in the perfect will of God. I knew that God had instructed me to act and He was shooting me out like an arrow from the Midwest to the West Coast.

I was excited to trust that God was directing my steps and giving me the instruction that I needed. Throughout the years He has pointed me back to this foundational verse about how He teaches us, through our simple yes, to trust in Him. When we trust Him, He teaches us what to do and how to do it.

> I will instruct you and teach you in the way you should go; I will guide you with My eye. Do not be like the horse *or* like the mule, *which* have no understanding, which must be harnessed with bit and bridle, else they will not come near you. Many sorrows *shall be* to the wicked; but he who trusts in the LORD, MERCY SHALL SURROUND HIM. Be glad in the LORD AND REJOICE, YOU RIGHTEOUS; and shout for joy, all *you* upright in heart!
>
> Psalm 32:8-11

The word *teach* in Hebrew is *yarah* (yah-rah) which has various meanings like instruct, direct, teach, point, shoot, aim, throw, and cast in a straight manner. The primary meaning of *yarah* is "to shoot straight." The most important Bible word derived from *yarah* is *Torah*, which refers to the *Law*. Although *torah* often translates as *law*, its meaning is "instruction," or, "teaching" (Spirit-Filled Life Bible, 780). The instruction Moses received from God for Israel is referred to as the Law of Moses.

I moved across the country by the instruction of the Lord to a place that I knew very little about—Redding, California—where I attended the Bethel School of Supernatural Ministry. At the time, I was unaware that I would complete all three years of ministry school, be asked to join the staff, and meet my amazing wife, Stefanie! I spent a total of eighteen years there, receiving hands-on training for my future. God was directing my steps, and He will direct your steps as well.

Learning to Serve

In those eighteen years, I had the opportunity to travel to every continent of the world (except Antarctica) to preach the Kingdom of God and Christ Jesus' saving and healing power that came through His death and resurrection. I had many opportunities to develop new outreach ministries as the Outreach Pastor at Bethel. Many of those ministries are still impacting the people in Redding, even though I no longer live there.

One of the outreach ministries I developed was called the Thanksgiving Feast. At the time, I was given the responsibility of overseeing a ministry house donated to Bethel for the purpose of discipling people from the community. Ten to twelve men—from the school and from the community—lived in the house at any given time. The students and I discipled the other men. One night while I slept, the Lord spoke to me about Chapter 58 in the book of Isaiah. God began to speak to me about "the chosen fast" in that chapter. He told me in the fall of 2001 to bring as many homeless people as I could to my house to feed them over the Thanksgiving holiday.

God's Word is a lamp to our feet, and when we obey His Word miracles start to happen. My desire and prayer were that my obedience would impact lives. As I studied Isaiah 58, God's instruction as to what I was to do became clear and practical. He wanted me to take people off the street and feed them in my house.

> *Is* this not the fast that I have chosen: to loose the bonds of wickedness, to undo the heavy burdens, to let the oppressed go free, and that you break every yoke? *Is it* not to share your bread with the hungry, and that you bring to your house the poor who are cast out; when you see the naked, that you cover him, and not hide yourself from your own flesh? Then your light shall break forth like the morning, your healing shall spring forth speedily, and your righteousness shall go before you; the glory of the LORD SHALL BE YOUR REAR GUARD. Then you shall call, and the LORD WILL ANSWER; you shall cry, and He

will say, 'Here I *am.*' If you take away the yoke from your midst, the pointing of the finger, and speaking wickedness, *if* you extend your soul to the hungry and satisfy the afflicted soul, then your light shall dawn in the darkness, and your darkness shall *be* as the noonday. The LORD WILL GUIDE YOU CONTINUALLY, and satisfy your soul in drought, and strengthen your bones; you shall be like a watered garden, and like a spring of water, whose waters do not fail. Those from among you shall build the old waste places; you shall raise up the foundations of many generations; and you shall be called the Repairer of the Breach, The Restorer of Streets to Dwell In. If you turn away your foot from the Sabbath, *From* doing your pleasure on My holy day, and call the Sabbath a delight, the holy *day* of the LORD HONORABLE, and shall honor Him, not doing your own ways, nor finding your own pleasure, nor speaking *your own* words, then you shall delight yourself in the LORD; and I will cause you to ride on the high hills of the earth, and feed you with the heritage of Jacob your father. The mouth of the LORD HAS SPOKEN.

Isaiah 58:6-14

I read these verses repeatedly after He gave them to me in the dream. God wanted the hurting and broken to come to my house for a meal and He promised that over a meal He would impact their lives. I wanted my life to shine and to see lives around me changed. I wanted to express a level of compassion that would not be afraid of people's mistakes or failures. I did not want to be politically correct; I just wanted to be a disciple of Jesus Christ who walked in faith and obedience.

I asked God how I could do this even though I did not have any money. He said, *Trust me.* I said to Him, *OK, I am just a student, and I don't know what to do. I don't have any money.* He told me to share the vision He had given me and to watch Him provide. I said that I would and so I shared the vision with Mark Brooks, the director of the ministry school. Mark still helps run the Bethel School of Ministry today. I asked him if I could share with the class and see if anyone would like to help. He gave me permission and so I shared the vision with my classmates. I was surprised to see the number of students that not only wanted to help feed the poor but who gave money they needed for themselves.

That year we fed one hundred and five people at the discipleship house. We had other students driving all around the city looking for the homeless to bring to our house. We turned our backyard into a dining room and treated them with love and honor. We had so much food that we gave away one hundred pies. We not only had enough food to feed everyone, we also had money left over from the donations. Those who donated agreed that I should use the rest of the money to go on a mission trip to Mexico, taking a man with me who used to live on the streets.

Through this experience, God showed me that by acknowledging and trusting Him, He was leading and guiding me and making my path clear. These are a few things that God taught me by obediently taking a step of faith and following the Leader.

1. He loves the homeless community so much—they are so deeply on His heart—that He will give us direction (or in my case, a dream) about how to practically serve and love them.
2. He does not always give us the full picture of what He is going to do. All I knew is that I was supposed to feed as many as I could that year at my house. I stepped out in faith and He took care of the rest.
3. He does not always give us the "next steps" until we take that first step of obedience. He did not tell me initially how to build a team that would help, that only came after I obeyed Him.
4. Faith-filled leadership is not about having a title but more about faith influence. I did not have a paid title with the homeless community, but very soon many of them saw me as their pastor, even though I was only in my early twenties.
5. We must act quickly in faith. If I had not acted quickly when He told me to move and when He told me to feed the homeless, I may have been talked out of obedience.
6. Although a dream is bigger than we can accomplish on our own, He gives us what we need to see it through. He gave me the vision to create a team to accomplish the Thanksgiving Feast.
7. A true vision from God will empower us with a passion for working extra hard to accomplish that vision.
8. Obedience positively impacts those around

us. My obedience positively impacted both the homeless community and many students who joined with me.

The Thanksgiving Feast has grown so much that Bethel Church now rents the local Veterans Hall to feed all the people from the community who come in search of a meal and some hope. Although I no longer lead this outreach, the seed of radical trust and obedience is still bearing fruit in the hearts and lives of those in need in Redding, California.

ONE
TWO
THREE
FOUR
FIVE
SIX
SEVEN
EIGHT
NINE

5
Obedient Faith

God is faithful. Just as water always seeks
and fills the lowest place, so the moment
God finds the creature humble and empty,
His glory and power flow in to raise up and
bless.

–Andrew Murray

Sometimes the places that God takes us are not always our first choice, but when we submit to Him, we come to realize that He knows what He is doing, and the best thing for us to do is to love Him and obey Him no matter what.

I was committed to lead two teams in Africa one summer. The plan was that I would take a team in early summer, do some crusades and power evangelism, and then return with a second team to do the same thing later that summer. Instead, everything was about to change because of a dream.

While on a ministry trip with Bill Johnson I had a dream that I was supposed to move to Weaverville, California that summer, the town where Bill used to pastor at Mountain Chapel. I woke up confused. I did not want to move there. I wanted to be in Africa. I already had things in motion with the teams and felt it would not be right to back out. I shared the dream with a few friends.

I kept asking myself, *what is there for me in Weaverville?* A few days went by, and I still had this nagging feeling that I was not to go to Africa but to Weaverville. I still did not want to go. One night before going to bed I got on my knees and prayed to God that if He wanted me to go to Weaverville for the summer instead of Africa, to please change my heart and that would be a sign that I was to go. When I woke up the next morning, I realized that my heart had changed. I wanted to move to Weaverville. I thanked the Lord and shared with friends and other leaders that were involved in the trips to Africa that I could not go that summer because I was to be in Weaverville.

Once I had chosen to move, I needed to find a summer job and a place to stay. I also needed to talk to Steve Backland, who was the pastor of Mountain Chapel at the time, to see if he would take me on as a summer intern. He agreed.

I did not know what to expect in my internship. Doing an internship with Steve was something I felt God was asking me to do. I think it is important to mention that God knows who we need as a mentor in certain seasons of our lives, in order to grow us into who He created us to be. Iron sharpens iron and God knew that I needed Steve to sharpen areas in my life. Steve has the gift of faith to see through the eyes of hope. If you don't have hope in specific areas of your life, it is likely that there is a lie that you believe about yourself or your situation that is influencing you.

Shortly after Steve accepted me into his summer internship at Mountain Chapel, I was offered a house for free for the entire summer. The owner of the home left me a key while he and his daughter spent the summer in Southern California. God set this up. He knew that I needed privacy because He was going to encounter me with love and power. I was amazed at how fast God opened doors for me in this little town. I soon landed a part time job at a local restaurant in the heart of downtown Weaverville.

Cleansing the Heart

Early in my internship, I was completely thrown off guard when Steve asked me if I knew how to use a computer. I told him no. I was a little frustrated at first when he asked me, because in my mind this had nothing to do with interning. He said that he wanted me to learn how to type and use a computer. *Really, God? Did you bring me up here for this?* Steve quickly got my attention when he told me that I never know if God might have me write books in the future, and I will need to know how to type. *Oh, ok!*

I did not have much responsibility other than leading a few different outreaches, so I found myself spending a large portion of the summer praying and studying the Word of God. I worked about eighteen to twenty hours a week at the restaurant washing dishes with a few young teenagers. It was very humbling because I had not done that kind of work since I was a teenager myself.

One night while washing dishes I started to complain silently in my heart to God. *Why am I here, Lord?* My attitude was very negative. *I could be in South Africa preaching the Gospel, but I am up here on this mountaintop washing dishes with some young teenagers.* Even though I made it a point to share my faith inside the workplace, my heart was grieving. I kept asking Him why I was there.

Suddenly the voice of God spoke loudly in my heart. *Chris, it took me getting you on this mountain to reach your heart. While you have been washing and scrubbing those dishes, I have been washing your heart. I had to do an in-reach with you before you did more outreach!* He went on to reveal what He was washing out of my heart and mind. I had recently broken up with a former girlfriend, choosing to step away from a relationship that I knew was not the best situation. It was something I had to do, but I would have delayed breaking up with her had I gone to South Africa. She was a great Christian girl, yet God kept speaking in my heart that she was not the best for me.

Along with the effects of my recent breakup, God had been working on my character concerning the unhealthy need for recognition. Fear of man revealed the lack of trust and security that I had in my relationship with Jesus. God knew that the fear of man, and a secret desire for recognition, had to be uprooted so that He could take me into a future He had planned for me; so that I would be able to do what He was going to ask of me. He knew that these childlike, inner behaviors had to be addressed to start the process of going deeper in my heart. He revealed it in that stunning moment while I washed dishes. *Ok, God, I am yours,* I thought. *Go deeply into my heart. I want to meet with you this summer, and now that I know what it is you want to do, I open myself to you. Have your way, Lord!*

I realized that the cleansing of our hearts is such an important part of our journey of faith. What does God want to wash out of your heart so that you can live the life of faith He has called you to live?

Growing in Faith

It was that summer that I learned how to use a computer and where I spent countless hours in prayer and studying the Bible. The fear of man and the opinions of people around me lost their controlling grip on my life. Please let me explain a little more about this. I did not fear their opinions when it came to sharing my faith; it had to do more with my perception of what spiritual leaders thought about me, and my overcompensation for recognition.

I was uncomfortable around leaders because I was often afraid of being rejected. I knew that the sting of growing up rejected by peers and adults still had adverse effects on me, even though I was an adult. I subconsciously started to manipulate some relationships out of fear. I thought that if I withdrew, then it would not hurt as much if they withdrew from me. In many ways, I felt like King Saul; he was already king but consistently forgot it because he feared that people were not with him or for him.

I realized that if I could not work it out in my heart, I would react from fear and do the same thing that he did; disobeying God in a time of pressure. Look at this passage in 1 Samuel 15:24, "Then Saul said to Samuel, 'I have sinned, for I have transgressed the commandment of the LORD and your words, be-

cause I feared the people and obeyed their voice.'"
It was the second time that Saul disobeyed the voice
of God under pressure. He feared the people and because of that, his calling and purpose were given to
David, a man who had the heart of God and would
not fear who was or was not with him. God took
me up to Mountain Chapel that summer because He
knew I needed to make future choices from a place
of faith and obedience instead of fear.

Experiencing Breakthrough

As I look back at that season on the mountain, I
learned many things that brought about life-altering
breakthrough and taught me about walking in obedient faith. Many of these were simple concepts that
had profound impact.

As you read through these, ask God to speak to you
about overcoming your own personal obstacles. I
encourage you to take time to look at each lesson
and resulting question. How can you apply these
to your own life and your personal breakthrough in
obedient faith?

1. I learned how to use a computer to ex-
    press myself and have written many
    books that have helped others.
    a. What skills and gifts can you devel-
        op today that could impact your life
        for years to come?
2. I learned how to let go of the fear of man
    and obey God even when I feel pressured
    to not obey Him.

      a. When have you felt pressured away from obedience to God? Do you struggle with the fear of man?

3. I learned how to put my faith and trust in God so that I do not settle in my heart. I began to believe that He knows everything about me, even when I would meet my future wife, Stefanie.

      a. What areas of your life do you need to place into God's hands? He knows everything about you and cares about every detail of your life!

4. I learned to operate in trust and confidence with other leaders instead of fear, even though I was younger and less experienced.

      a. What areas of your life need a boost in trust and confidence? How is fear preventing you from walking in trust?

5. I learned to have a healthy perspective on life and what God has called me to do without the distraction of other's opinions about my life.

      a. Ask God what He is saying about your purpose in life. His perspective brings clarity and direction!

6. I learned to obey God and not question Him when He called me to do something that did not make sense in the moment.

      a. Is there anything God is speaking to you that does not make sense? What would it look like to step out in faith and obedience in this area?

7. I learned that God knows how to provide

for everything that He has called me to do.

    a. Consider all the ways in which God has provided for you in the past. Let my testimony and your experience increase your faith that God will always provide for you!

8.   I learned that the Christian life has way more to do with my heart than my gifts. God loves us so much that He will slow us down and prune our hearts so that we bear long-term fruit.

    a. What is God doing in your heart right now? His work in your life demonstrates His profound love for you!

9.   I learned that God knows the people I need in my life to learn life's lessons. God used Steve as a divine instrument for my spiritual and practical growth.

    a. Who in your life is helping you grow both spiritually and practically? Ask God if there is anyone you need to connect with or learn from.

10.   I learned that promotion in life does not always look the way I hope it looks. Working at the restaurant felt like a setback, but from God's perspective it was a promotion of the heart, which is more valuable that any amount of money I could have earned that summer. I experienced true riches that only come through faith in God.

    a. What promotions have you experienced that felt like setbacks as you walked through them? How does that influence the way you approach your life today?

Obedient faith often looks like stepping into unknown situations and places we never imagined we would go. By walking in obedience to God, I received breakthrough in many different areas of my life. The truth is that our breakthrough enables a breakthrough in others. I bless you to walk in obedient faith and see your life changed from the inside out. Breakthrough is available to you!

ONE

TWO

THREE

FOUR

FIVE

SIX

SEVEN

EIGHT

NINE

6

Active Faith

We are all faced with a series of great opportunities brilliantly disguised as impossible situations.

–Chuck Swindoll

When I first launched our ministry, Compassion To Action, God asked me to do something that far exceeded our ministry's resources and capacity. At the time, Compassion to Action only had about five hundred dollars in the bank. God spoke to me in a vision to hold a stadium seating event in Portland, Oregon that would require nearly one million dollars. Faith is not always practical. It was not practical to book a convention center when I had only five hundred dollars in our bank account! I knew if I was going to do what God had called me to do, I had to consistently hear Him speak to my heart and I had to meditate on His Word so that fear would not have control.

Stay True to the Vision

After I received the vision for the Portland 2018 stadium event, I prayed about it for two months so that I would have a gift of faith (1 Corinthians 12:9) before I shared it with anyone else. I had a feeling that there might be people who would try to dissuade me from such a large undertaking. God was leading me to lay a strong foundation in faith so that I would not back down, be swayed, or change the vision He had given me.

After the gift of faith came, I had to take practical steps of faith that acknowledged the larger vision I had of stadium seating events across America. The first place I saw was Portland. In the vision, I could hear the prayers of the saints in my heart, and not only could I hear it, but it was also as though I could feel them as well. It was important that I acknowledged the prayers of the saints when I met with people.

Throughout the planning stages, I checked in with the Lord consistently to make sure that I was not drifting away from His vision. If I stayed true to the vision, God would stay true to His Word. His Word is the provision and the operational power to see the fulfillment of the Word when we follow it.

Take Courage

Throughout this process, I learned that the eyes of my heart needed to see through faith, not fear. My constant prayer was, *Lord, give me courage. Lord, I would rather be a man of courage than a coward that shrinks back in fear.*

> This Book of the Law shall not depart from your mouth, but you shall meditate in it day

and night, that you may observe to do according to all that is written in it. For then you will make your way prosperous, and then you will have good success. Have I not commanded you? Be strong and of good courage; do not be afraid, nor be dismayed, for the LORD your God *is* with you wherever you go.

Joshua 1:8-9

It takes courage and faith to do what you know God is calling you to do, even when you feel afraid. Courage is not the absence of the emotion of fear. It is the commitment never to bow down and surrender to fear. Throughout the Bible, we see people that faced fear but had an unwavering commitment to obey God, which led them on the path of courage. Their courage inspired others to trust God and to believe in Him. These past heroes of the faith are still speaking to us through their stories. In your own study time, I encourage you to study these men and women of God in the Bible: Ruth, Joshua, Caleb, Moses, Abraham, Sara, Nehemiah, David, Noah, Gideon, Isaiah, Elijah, Elisha, Deborah, Peter, Paul, Stephen, and Jesus in the gospels.

Like Moses, I felt called to go to a place I did not know, and as I stepped out in faith to pursue the vision God had given me for Portland 2018, He heard my prayer for courage. I greatly needed courage for the road ahead. Some people did, in fact, try to discourage me from what God had called me to do. At times I felt like Nehemiah, especially when Sanballat and Tobiah came against him. Nehemiah sought to fulfill his vision of rebuilding the wall in Jerusalem, but he constantly faced the dissension of Sanballat and Tobiah.

> But when Sanballat the Horonite, Tobiah the Ammonite official, and Geshem the Arab heard *of it,* they laughed at us and despised us, and said, "What *is* this thing that you are doing? Will you rebel against the king?" So I answered them, and said to them, "The God of heaven Himself will prosper us; therefore we His servants will arise and build, but you have no heritage or right or memorial in Jerusalem."

> Nehemiah 2:19-20

Nehemiah needed great strength and endurance to challenge the dissension coming against him. That is what I needed as well. Just like Nehemiah, God gave me a gift of faith and courage so that I would not back down and disobey the Lord.

When God asks you to do something, He desires to do it with you. When you hear a call from God, He is inviting you to a deeper level of trust and intimacy with Him. Obedience reveals the heart. Taking an active step of faith and obeying Him, even when we don't fully understand or we feel fear, reveals that our hearts truly love and trust Jesus. When God called Moses to lead the children of Israel out of Egypt, Moses was terrified. He could have run or said no to the call. But he said yes when he realized he was not doing it by his strength but by the power and the authority of God that came with the mission and the assignment.

When we say yes to the call of God, we step out of our natural ability and into His supernatural empowerment. Obedience brings us into realms of His favor, grace, and power that we can never experience on our own. Whatever chapter of your story you are in, know that the author of faith is with you, and He is imparting His courage to your heart along the journey.

I noticed that my heart's true contents revealed themselves through times of testing when I was faced with the challenge of obeying God's Word. How I responded in faith—the action I chose to take—showed what was really in my heart. Through times of uncertainty and testing, it is essential for our hearts to continually give thanks to God, acknowledging and declaring His faithfulness night and day. My prayer for you is that you realize that Jesus is with you building your faith in every season of your life. No matter how you feel, He will give you the courage and the strength to stay true to His Word and walk in active faith with Him through any circumstance.

ONE
TWO
THREE
FOUR
FIVE
SIX
SEVEN
EIGHT
NINE

7

Faith that Pleases God

If we displease God, does it matter whom we please? If we please Him does it matter whom we displease?

—Leonard Ravenhill

Faith is more valuable than gold or silver or any sum of money, for it is what pleases God. Through the grace of the Gospel of Jesus Christ, we come into faith, and it is a gift of God. This gift grows as we steward well the measure of faith that God has given us. It is important that we develop the gift He so graciously gives. In the Bible, Jesus tells the following story about the importance of being faithful to steward what God has given.

> For *the kingdom of heaven is* like a man traveling to a far country, *who* called his own servants and delivered his goods to them. And to one he gave five talents, to another two, and to another one, to each according to his own ability; and immediately he went on a journey. Then he who had received the five talents went and traded with them, and made another five talents. And likewise he who *had received* two gained two more also. But he who had received one went and

dug in the ground, and hid his lord's money. After a long time the lord of those servants came and settled accounts with them. So he who had received five talents came and brought five other talents, saying, "Lord, you delivered to me five talents; look, I have gained five more talents besides them." His lord said to him, "Well *done,* good and faithful servant; you were faithful over a few things, I will make you ruler over many things. Enter into the joy of your lord." He also who had received two talents came and said, "Lord, you delivered to me two talents; look, I have gained two more talents besides them." His lord said to him, "Well *done,* good and faithful servant; you have been faithful over a few things, I will make you ruler over many things. Enter into the joy of your lord." Then he who had received the one talent came and said, "Lord, I knew you to be a hard man, reaping where you have not sown, and gathering where you have not scattered seed. And I was afraid, and went and hid your talent in the ground. Look, *there* you have *what is* yours." But his lord answered and said to him, "You wicked and lazy servant, you knew that I reap where I have not sown, and gather where I have not scattered seed. So you ought to have deposited my money with the bankers, and at my coming I would have received back my own with interest. So take the talent from him, and give *it* to him who has ten talents. For to everyone who has, more will be given, and he will have abundance; but from him who does not have, even what he has will be taken away. And cast the unprofitable servant into the outer darkness. There will be weeping and gnashing of teeth."

Matthew 25:14-30

In this story, the master distributed different amounts of money to his servants. He trusted them with its management and growth. He gave five talents to one, two talents to another, and one talent to the last servant. They had the freedom to use their unique abilities to manage their money.

The same is true of the faith and the gifts we have been given. Many people ask for more faith. Asking for more faith is good, but God looks at our ability to make use of what He has already given us. In the parable, the master asks his servants what they did with what he gave them. The servant who received five talents used his money to make five more talents. The second servant also used his two talents to double the yield. Their yields increased through their faithfulness to use and grow them well. The response of the master in Matthew 25:23 is a picture of God our Father when we live a life of faith, "Well *done*, good and faithful servant; you have been faithful over a few things, I will make you ruler over many things. Enter into the joy of your lord." We all want to hear our Father say, *Well done. I am proud of you. You did well.* Words of affirmation from the Father build a fortress of confidence and faith in our hearts. The servants' faithfulness ushered them into joyful communion with their lord.

This parable is such a clear picture of how we can

stay in joyful communion with God. Many people think that the joy of the Lord is an event, like when Holy laughter breaks out during worship. But true joy comes from the Holy Spirit, and it is never meant to last just one night. True joy comes when you are faithful to do and be what God has called you to do and be. A deep sense of pleasure and joy flows from your heart when you lay your head down at night knowing you have stewarded well God's gracious gift to live by faith.

Faith Overcomes Fear

When the master returned, in the parable, he asked the servant who was given one talent what he did with it. The servant had an opportunity to bring an increase to his talent, but he allowed fear to control him. Instead of being faithful, he bowed to fear and became lazy. He despised what was given to him for free, and instead of putting the money in the bank, he decided to hide it. It illustrates what fear does to people. They belittle what they have been given to excuse why they are disobedient and unfaithful with it.

It is important to understand that fear is a spirit, not a personality type. There are many spirits of fear that talk to people. I know very well what it is like to run into a spirit of fear. But I have learned over time that just because I feel fear does not mean I have to bow down to it. When you face fear, it means that there is a breakthrough on the other side of that wall. Fear knows this, and this evil spirit tries to hold you back from your destiny. The Bible warns us three hundred sixty-five times not to fear. Fear has the potential to knock on our hearts every day of the year. God is pleased when we remain faithful in the face of fear, and we push forward instead of shrinking back.

The very thing the lazy servant tried to hold on to because of fear was taken away from him and given to the servant with ten talents. Fear tells you to hold on to your life and stay in charge, but faith tells you to trust God and to surrender to whatever He calls you to do. Fear says, *This is my life.* But faith says, *It is no longer I who live but Christ who lives in me!*

> I have been crucified with Christ; it is no longer I who live, but Christ lives in me; and the *life* which I now live in the flesh I live by faith in the Son of God, who loved me and gave Himself for me.
>
> Galatians 2:20

The master cast the unfaithful servant into outer darkness. Fear tells you that it is keeping you safe, but it is luring you to destruction. As we are warned in Matthew 25:30, there will be anguish, or weeping and gnashing of teeth for those who live a life ruled by fear. However, there is the promise of great joy and celebration in store for those who live in faith.

Faithfulness Brings Increase

I sometimes tell my daughter, Brielle, to pick up

her toys and put them away. But my wife, Stefanie, says, "Chris, you have to show Brielle what you mean by demonstrating it first. Then you have to do it with her for her to learn to do it on her own in the future."

When we are newly born again, God sees us like little children. He teaches us how much He loves us, how we can obey Him, and how we can overcome fear through obedience. He teaches us His will through His Word, and He demonstrates how to obey Him by displaying it through the life of Jesus and the lives of the believers around us.

My daughter needed me to demonstrate and teach her what I meant when I told her to pick up her toys and put them away. In the last two years, she has grown dramatically, and now she obeys me when I ask her to do something like pick up her toys. I know it is an elementary example, but when I see my little girl obey me and my wife, it brings joy to my heart. I know that if she learns to be faithful to what her parents teach her, it will help her learn to obey God.

Learning to obey God requires faithfulness. I remember barely having enough money to buy deodorant on a sweltering summer day in California. All I had left was five dollars. I was walking out of a gas station when I saw a man in a run-down car counting some change. As I walked by, the Holy Spirit said to me, *Chris, give him your last five dollars.* I said out of fear, *God, this is all I have. I don't want to.* In my mind, I judged the man and figured he would probably spend the money on alcohol. But He spoke to me again, *Go give him your last five dollars!*

My heart was stubborn, and I tried to convince God that I had a better plan. Once again, God did not budge, and I was not changing His mind. He said again, *Go and give him the money.* Finally, I surrendered and said, *Fine, I will.* As I walked up to his car, my heart softened, and I said, "Excuse me, sir, I wanted to tell you that Jesus loves you and has a plan for your life. He wanted me to give you my last five dollars." In shock and amazement, he said, "You have no idea how much this means to me! I was counting all the change that I have left to see if I had enough money to buy milk for my babies. Thank you so much." I watched this man's entire countenance change, and as I walked away, I felt God's pleasure. Then He spoke to me clearly that by giving away my last five dollars, I would receive full funding for the mission trip that I wanted to go on but could not afford. A short time later, I received a donation that enabled me to go on that mission trip.

As I look back and reflect on this story, the joy that I experienced after I gave away the five dollars was worth more than any amount of money I could have received. I felt God's love so strongly for that man. I learned two important lessons: to obey God right away and not to judge others. When we are young in faith, the voice of the Lord is new and unfamiliar, and so is stepping out in faith. The more mature we become and the more we learn to recognize God's voice, the more we are required to walk in quick and faithful obedience.

In the example of my daughter, it is normal to need to teach a two-year-old to pick up her toys, but if I still need to teach her how to pick up after herself when she is eighteen, something is wrong with her development. The same is true in our relationship with the Father.

I shared the story about the five dollars purposely because when you talk about money and faithfulness, it cuts right to the heart. There have been numerous times that God has asked me to do something to financially bless someone else that did not make sense in the natural. Sometimes I think, *Why? Don't you know I have a need as well, Lord?* That is the voice of fear that only sees from a natural perspective. I must admit that there have been many times that I have only seen from the natural perspective. When God asks you to do something, never plan to do it with what is in your hands but with what is in His hands.

There was a time when I had acquired enough funds to get out of debt. It was something that I had worked on for years. But instead of paying off that debt, God spoke to my heart to give the funds away. I shared this impression with my wife. I needed confirmation from her since these hard-earned funds had the potential to get us out of major debt. After prayer, we felt the right thing to do was to give the entire revenue stream to another ministry and to entrust ourselves to God. When I surrendered, joy came into my heart, and I knew that I was doing the right thing, even though others counseled me not to do it. I knew with my whole heart that I had to.

After a year went by, I was still in debt. As a young married man, I desired to provide a house for my wife since she dreamed of having a home. I did not know how I was going to be able to do this with the debt that we had. But God knew our need, and He had the best timing, even though it was not the timing that I wanted. He sent someone into our lives who sowed into us on an annual basis to help get us out of debt. It enabled us to buy our first home. After God put this man in our lives, He reminded me of my act of obedience to give away the revenue that I had worked so hard to earn.

As I looked back on my life, I saw a trail of God's blessings that came from radical steps of faithful obedience. These blessings were more valuable than money, and the ripple effect from just one act of obedience made that original sacrifice look very small in comparison.

The truth is that when you are faithful with a little, God will give you more. But the real test is, when He gives you more, does the abundance define you? Does it prevent you from obeying Jesus because you love what He gives you more than you love the One who gave it to you? With increase comes great responsibility to stay faithful. When God gives you something, it is because He is a Father who trusts you and believes in you.

My prayer for you is that your life, through faithfulness and good stewardship, brings glory to God and impacts a generation to know Jesus and faithfully follow Him no matter the cost. I pray that in doing this, you experience the joy and the pleasure of God in an ever-increasing measure.

ONE
TWO
THREE
FOUR
FIVE
SIX
SEVEN
EIGHT
NINE

8
Faith for the Harvest

Do you not say, "There are still four
months and then comes the harvest?"
Behold, I say to you, lift up your eyes and
look at the fields, for they are already white
for harvest!

–John 4:35

One year, as it was approaching harvest time, I had
the privilege of hanging out with some friends on
their farm. They shared the wisdom they had acquired over years of farming during harvest season.
They explained that when harvest time came, they
would need every working hand. There is more
work to be done on a farm during harvest than there
is the rest of the year. As a farmer, it is essential to
know the season you are in so that you know what
work needs to be done. Jesus exemplified this prin-
ciple, showing us the importance of recognizing
the season. Throughout the gospels and through the
book of Acts we see Jesus and His disciples looking
through the eyes of faith for the harvest of souls.

Eyes to See the Harvest

In John chapter 4, Jesus asked the woman at the

well for a drink of water. Through their conversation, Jesus revealed to her that while she had a physical need for water, she had a spiritual need for living water that is eternal life in Jesus. In their short conversation this woman's life turned upside down. After one life-changing encounter with Him, she told her village about the man named Jesus, the Messiah. Jesus so deeply impacted her that she became the first female evangelist in the Bible! She gathered the people of her city to come and listen to Jesus, and after listening to Him, they believed in Him for themselves.

> And many of the Samaritans of that city believed in Him because of the word of the woman who testified, "He told me all that I *ever* did." So, when the Samaritans had come to Him, they urged Him to stay with them; and He stayed there two days. And many more believed because of His own word. Then they said to the woman, "Now we believe, not because of what you said, for we ourselves have heard *Him* and we know that this is indeed the Christ, the Savior of the world."

> John 4:39-42

When Jesus' disciples came and joined Him at the well, they tried to get Him to eat. But Jesus told them He was already feasting because His food was to do the will of God. Both the woman and the disciples focused on their physical needs for water and food, but Jesus had His eyes fixed on eternity. He saw people's eternal need for salvation and to live lives of obedience. Jesus knew that it was harvest time, so He knew the work He needed to do. From His heavenly perspective, Jesus had faith for the harvest of souls. Throughout His time on earth, He also called His disciples to a higher perspective. He told them to look up and see that the harvest was ripe. He imparted faith that the harvest was not a future event but a present season that required all hands-on deck.

Recently, I had a dream of a young man who wanted to go fishing. He had a small net, and it did not look like he was prepared to catch anything, but he had great anticipation that he was going to catch a fish. To my surprise and amazement, as I turned around, I saw him reel in a massive fish! Afterward, as I began to pray into this dream, the Lord spoke to me about the rising faith in this young generation who will lead in the harvest.

Around the same time, I had a dream about individuals who resembled David and Goliath from the Bible. In the dream, fear tried to prevent this young David from taking down the giant. He was almost ready to give up when suddenly a gift of faith came on him. His fear was transformed into an exciting opportunity to step into his destiny and take down this giant. These two dreams revealed the kind of faith that the Lord is giving to the Church right now. The Lord is raising a generation that will step out to preach the Gospel, even if they feel afraid or unprepared. They will step out in faith, and the Lord will use them to bring in a massive harvest of souls.

The Harvest is Here

The Lord is already stirring great faith for the harvest in this nation. I want to encourage you with the testimonies of those who are beginning to step out and share the Gospel for the first time. I recently heard the story of a young woman who works for a company that provides transportation to its customers. In three weeks, this young woman started sharing the message of Jesus Christ and powerfully impacted over fifty passengers! Another testimony comes from a young sixteen-year-old girl named Ava who attended Compassion To Action's Portland 2018 stadium event. Here is her story:

> A few days ago, I was out ministering with the Compassion To Action team. I was evangelizing with one of the CTA team members, Mitchell. I saw two girls walking by. I felt the Lord tug on my heart and tell me to go after them. The first girl's name was Cheryl. It was significant because I had recently watched the movie Finger of God 2. The movie inspired me to go out and share Jesus, and I asked God to give me a name. I heard the Holy Spirit say, *Cheryl*. I asked these two girls if they knew Jesus. They did not. However, they allowed us to pray for them. We prayed and prophesied over them, and we received a word of knowledge for Cheryl. After we gave her the word, she was able to release

forgiveness to some people who had hurt her deeply. Cheryl was able to feel the presence of Jesus for the first time. We prayed for peace over her heart, and Cheryl accepted Jesus. I was so wrecked. It was the first time I had ever led someone to Jesus!

The harvest is ripe and ready, and I cannot think of anything more exciting than seeing people get equipped to lead others to salvation, healing, and deliverance from evil spirits. The harvest is ready and ripe, and my prayer is that you would see the opportunities that are placed right in front of you and that you would respond with the compassion of Jesus to seek out the ones that God is calling you to reach for Him. Let us have faith for the harvest.

ONE
TWO
THREE
FOUR
FIVE
SIX
SEVEN
EIGHT
NINE

9
God Wants to Use You

The Evangelistic Harvest is always urgent. The destiny of men and of nations is always being decided. Every generation is strategic. We are not responsible for the past generation, and we cannot bear the full responsibility for the next one; but we do have our generation. God will hold us responsible as to how well we fulfill our responsibilities to this age and take advantage of our opportunities.

–Billy Graham

When I lived in Redding, we wanted to make an impact in our city, and I felt faith to start going into nightclubs. I knew in my heart that the Holy Spirit was the greatest evangelist and that He wanted to use every believer to do great things in dark places. The more I prayed about it, the more I felt the Lord leading me to build a team that would start going into the nightclubs to reach people for Jesus. Jesus was speaking in my heart that in His sight, the people we would encounter at the clubs were like treasures that were living in darkness and desperately needed the love and the power of the Gospel to shine on them.

I gathered a team, and we established some core

values. We decided not to drink at the nightclubs because we did not want to create any stumbling blocks for people. I sought out people who were secure and solid in their identity in Jesus Christ and who also shared a vision to reach people for Jesus outside the four walls of the church. As the team and I began to go into nightclubs sharing the simple and powerful message of Jesus Christ, many people began to get saved, healed, and delivered.

One night the team met a young man named Justin. Justin had a lot to drink that night, and he wanted to know why our team was there. One lady, named Anne, told him that they loved Jesus and that they were there telling people about His love. He asked them what kind of church they went to, and Anne did not know what to say. Suddenly, God TV came on a screen right there in the nightclub, and there was a worship leader named Misty Edwards leading worship! Anne was shocked that this came on the screen at that exact moment. She pointed to the screen and said, "We go to a church like that!" After they began sharing with Justin, the Holy Spirit came powerfully to reveal Jesus Christ to him.

Standing there in a dark nightclub, the light of Jesus pierced the darkness and touched his heart. Justin surrendered his life to Jesus that night. The team invited him to come to church the following Sunday. At church, he had another radical encounter with Jesus Christ. Justin's life underwent an amazing transformation as he began to understand that Jesus is real, and that He died and rose again to save him. Justin began to forgive the people in his life, and the following week he was baptized. He signed up to go to ministry school three months later. Justin's mom was so impacted by what had happened to her son that she also went to ministry school the following year and ended up traveling with me to Africa. Many more testimonies took place as our nightclub team stepped out in faith as workers in the harvest.

Called to Minister

When I was a young believer, I used to think that God only wanted to use the people on the stage with the microphone to do great things for Him. But after reading the book of Acts and hearing testimonies of God using anyone who simply believed, my faith began to grow that He wants to use all of us. I hope and pray that even now as you read this book, God is stirring your spirit to see through eyes of faith that He wants to use you for the harvest. God wants to use you more than you want Him to use you. The harvest time is now, and God is stirring the hearts of His people to believe Him for greater things.

My friend Chuck is a banker, and I have heard him share story after story of people getting saved at his bank in Minnesota. People would sit down at his desk just looking to take out a loan or start a checking account, but as Chuck would talk with them, compassion and faith would stir in his heart. In the middle of his meetings, the Lord would suddenly give him words of encouragement and words of knowledge that came from the Holy Spirit for his clients. Sometimes he would feel led to ask them questions about their life, establishing trust between them. Then he would start to share the Gospel with them and as he did, all of heaven would pour out over that bank. Over the years, Chuck not only saw his bank grow financially, but he saw over eighty people surrender their lives to Jesus Christ!

> The Spirit of the Lord GOD *is* upon Me, because the LORD has anointed Me to preach good tidings to the poor; He has sent Me to heal the brokenhearted, to proclaim liberty to the captives, and the opening of the prison to *those who are* bound; to proclaim the acceptable year of the LORD, and the day of vengeance of our God; to comfort all who mourn, to console those who mourn in Zion, to give them beauty for ashes, the oil of joy for mourning, the garment of praise for the spirit of heaviness; that they may be called trees of righteousness, the planting of the LORD, that He may be glorified.
>
> Isaiah 61:1-3

The anointing of God is the Spirit of God resting on your life for the work of ministry. It is important for us to understand that we cannot bring someone to Jesus in our own power. But we can have faith that the message of the Gospel has the power to save, heal, and deliver. There are many voices and distractions that try to prevent us from sharing our faith. I was recently talking to a young man in Argentina while on a Compassion To Action mission trip. He saw God moving through our team and he got so excited that he started to step out in faith by praying for people in public. He admits that there was a war in his intellect and his heart about whether or not God would use him. Maybe you, too, can relate to this struggle.

As he shared, the young man started to tear up. He said, "Why have I allowed so many years to go by not doing anything?" It was then that he realized that God loved him and wanted to use him. At the same time, he felt God's love for people, which became a major motivation in his life. He admitted that after the evangelism conference, he thought the excitement and motivation were going to wear off. When the conference was over, however, he found himself being continually used by God, which confirmed to him that God really did want to use him to reach others.

"How can I keep this passion to reach people?" he asked me. I said, "I will share with you a few simple keys that will help you. First, stay connected to Jesus through prayer." I shared the importance of developing a lifelong prayer commitment. In prayer, your heart stays soft and you begin to feel the heart of God for people and their situations. When you feel God's heart for people it causes you to seek Him more, and this is truly one of the ways that you get to know Him.

The second thing I told him was to study God's Word consistently in order to find out His promises and His will. By doing this, our minds are renewed. I am a strong believer in meditating on the Word of God and memorizing it. The last thing that I shared with him was to be quick to obey whatever God tells you to do no matter how small or big it may be.

Surrendered to Faith

There are indicators that distinguish those who grow spiritually and those who stay stagnant. There is a lack of growth when we choose not to read the Word or apply it to our lives. We become stuck, as well, when we hear God's Word spoken to us and refuse to act because of fear. Growth, however, comes through reading the Word and asking God for an opportunity to demonstrate His Kingdom. Growth comes from hearing God's request and responding yes because of our love for Jesus and our commitment to follow Him no matter what happens.

Life is a gift and seeing through the eyes of faith is essential as we navigate through life and its challenges. Jesus never told His Church that everything would be easy. In fact, He promised that there would be hardship at times, an important reason to keep our eyes on Him. Life is a journey and not a sprint, but it is always meant to be lived in surrender to faith.

Faith does not back down during struggle or even amid feasting when everything seems fine. We need faith in every season in our lives so that we can see the way that God sees, and take the steps that are required of us to inherit the promises of God over our lives.

I believe in you and the call of God on your life and it is my prayer that you never waver or surrender to a life of unbelief, but that you would take your stand in history as one who believed God and walked with God through faith, a faith that sees from heaven's perspective.

One Hundred Bible Verses About Faith

From the very beginning of my journey and walk with God, I spent time reading, praying, memorizing, and declaring the Word of God. The Word is powerful and life-giving! As you continue to grow in faith and pursue God's heart, I encourage you to take time to feast on these verses. Let them encourage you and be a catalyst for your journey of radical, powerful faith that leads you to obey Him!

~Chris Overstreet

"And whatever things you ask in prayer, believing, you will receive" (Matthew 21:22).

So then faith *comes* by hearing, and hearing by the word of God (Romans 10:17).

But without faith *it is* impossible to please *Him,* for he who comes to God must believe that He is, and *that* He is a rewarder of those who diligently seek Him (Hebrews 11:6).

Now faith is the substance of things hoped for, the evidence of things not seen (Hebrews 11:1).

You believe that there is one God. You do well. Even the demons believe—and tremble! (James 2:19).

"For with God nothing will be impossible" (Luke 1:37).

Trust in the LORD WITH ALL YOUR HEART, and lean not on your own understanding; In all your ways acknowledge Him, and He shall direct your paths (Proverbs 3:5-6).

For by grace you have been saved through faith, and that not of yourselves; *it is* the gift of God (Ephesians 2:8).

That your faith should not be in the wisdom of men but in the power of God (1 Corinthians 2:5).

For God so loved the world that He gave His only begotten Son, that whoever believes in Him should not perish but have everlasting life (John 3:16).

I can do all things through Christ who strengthens me (Philippians 4:13).

You see then that a man is justified by works, and not by faith only (James 2:24).

And the apostles said to the Lord, "Increase our

faith" (Luke 17:5).

Jesus said to him, "If you can believe, all things *are* possible to him who believes" (Mark 9:23).

So Jesus said to them, "Because of your unbelief; for assuredly, I say to you, if you have faith as a mustard seed, you will say to this mountain, 'Move from here to there,' and it will move; and nothing will be impossible for you" (Matthew 17:20).

For I say, through the grace given to me, to everyone who is among you, not to think *of himself* more highly than he ought to think, but to think soberly, as God has dealt to each one a measure of faith (Romans 12:3).

I have been crucified with Christ; it is no longer I who live, but Christ lives in me; and the *life* which I now live in the flesh I live by faith in the Son of God, who loved me and gave Himself for me (Galatians 2:20).

Be still, and know that I *am* God; I will be exalted among the nations, I will be exalted in the earth! (Psalm 46:10).

I have fought the good fight, I have finished the race, I have kept the faith (2 Timothy 4:7).

And now abide faith, hope, love, these three; but the greatest of these *is* love (1 Corinthians 13:13).

Knowing that a man is not justified by the works of the law but by faith in Jesus Christ, even we have believed in Christ Jesus, that we might be justified by faith in Christ and not by the works of the law; for by the works of the law no flesh shall be justified (Galatians 2:16).

"Therefore I said to you that you will die in your sins; for if you do not believe that I am *He*, you will die in your sins" (John 8:24).

For whatever is born of God overcomes the world. And this is the victory that has overcome the world—our faith (1 John 5:4).

By faith Noah, being divinely warned of things not yet seen, moved with godly fear, prepared an ark for the saving of his household, by which he condemned the world and became heir of the righteousness which is according to faith (Hebrews 11:7).

Above all, taking the shield of faith with which you will be able to quench all the fiery darts of the wicked one (Ephesians 6:16).

He who believes and is baptized will be saved; but he who does not believe will be condemned (Mark 16:16).

Then Jesus said to him, "Go your way; your faith has made you well." And immediately he received his sight and followed Jesus on the road (Mark 10:52).

That if you confess with your mouth the Lord Jesus and believe in your heart that God has raised Him from the dead, you will be saved (Romans 10:9).

So Jesus answered and said to them, "Assuredly, I say to you, if you have faith and do not doubt, you will not only do what was done to the fig tree, but also if you say to this mountain, 'Be removed and be cast into the sea,' it will be done" (Matthew 21:21).

"Behold the proud, his soul is not upright in him; but the just shall live by his faith" (Habakkuk 2:4).

Watch, stand fast in the faith, be brave, be strong (1 Corinthians 16:13).

Thus also faith by itself, if it does not have works, is dead (James 2:17).

Now may the God of hope fill you with all joy and peace in believing, that you may abound in hope by the power of the Holy Spirit (Romans 15:13).

He did not waver at the promise of God through

unbelief, but was strengthened in faith, giving glory to God, and being fully convinced that what He had promised He was also able to perform (Romans 4:20-21).

Fight the good fight of faith, lay hold on eternal life, to which you were also called and have confessed the good confession in the presence of many witnesses (1 Timothy 6:12).

But He said, "The things which are impossible with men are possible with God" (Luke 18:27).

"He who believes in the Son has everlasting life; and he who does not believe the Son shall not see life, but the wrath of God abides on him" (John 3:36).

Knowing that the testing of your faith produces patience (James 1:3).

In the beginning was the Word, and the Word was with God, and the Word was God (John 1:1).

But let him ask in faith, with no doubting, for he who doubts is like a wave of the sea driven and tossed by the wind (James 1:6).

"No one can serve two masters; for either he will

hate the one and love the other, or else he will be loyal to the one and despise the other. You cannot serve God and mammon" (Matthew 6:24).

Looking unto Jesus, the author and finisher of *our* faith, who for the joy that was set before Him endured the cross, despising the shame, and has sat down at the right hand of the throne of God (Hebrews 12:2).

And Jesus said to them, "I am the bread of life. He who comes to Me shall never hunger, and he who believes in Me shall never thirst" (John 6:35).

But sanctify the Lord God in your hearts, and always *be* ready to *give* a defense to everyone who asks you a reason for the hope that is in you, with meekness and fear (1 Peter 3:15).

Therefore I say to you, whatever things you ask when you pray, believe that you receive *them,* and you will have *them* (Mark 11:24).

Then Jesus answered and said to her, "O woman, great *is* your faith! Let it be to you as you desire." And her daughter was healed from that very hour (Matthew 15:28).

The LORD *is* my shepherd; I shall not want. He makes me to lie down in green pastures; He leads me beside the still waters. He restores my soul; He leads me in the paths of righteousness for His name's sake. Yea, though I walk through the valley of the shadow of death, I will fear no evil; for You *are* with me; your rod and Your staff, they comfort me. You prepare a table before me in the presence of my enemies; you anoint my head with oil; my cup runs over. Surely goodness and mercy shall follow me all the days of my life; and I will dwell in the house of the LORD forever (Psalm 23).

Whoever believes that Jesus is the Christ is born of God, and everyone who loves Him who begot also loves him who is begotten of Him (1 John 5:1).

And though I have *the gift of* prophecy, and understand all mysteries and all knowledge, and though I have all faith, so that I could remove mountains, but have not love, I am nothing (1 Corinthians 13:2).

So Jesus answered and said to them, "Have faith in God" (Mark 11:22).

But someone will say, "You have faith, and I have works." Show me your faith without your works, and I will show you my faith by my works (James 2:18).

For I am not ashamed of the gospel of Christ, for it is the power of God to salvation for everyone who believes, for the Jew first and also for the Greek. For in it the righteousness of God is revealed from faith to faith; as it is written, "The just shall live by faith" (Romans 1:16-17).

That the genuineness of your faith, *being* much more precious than gold that perishes, though it is tested by fire, may be found to praise, honor, and glory at the revelation of Jesus Christ (1 Peter 1:7).

But the fruit of the Spirit is love, joy, peace, long-suffering, kindness, goodness, faithfulness (Galatians 5:22).

But as many as received Him, to them He gave the right to become children of God, to those who believe in His name (John 1:12).

No temptation has overtaken you except such as is common to man; but God *is* faithful, who will not allow you to be tempted beyond what you are able, but with the temptation will also make the way of escape, that you may be able to bear *it* (1 Corinthians 10:13).

For I know the thoughts that I think toward you, says the Lord, thoughts of peace and not of evil, to give you a future and a hope (JEREMIAH 29:11).

Therefore, having been justified by faith, we

have peace with God through our Lord Jesus Christ, through whom also we have access by faith into this grace in which we stand, and rejoice in hope of the glory of God. And not only *that,* but we also glory in tribulations, knowing that tribulation produces perseverance; and perseverance, character; and character, hope. Now hope does not disappoint, because the love of God has been poured out in our hearts by the Holy Spirit who was given to us (Romans 5:1-5).

But he who doubts is condemned if he eats, because *he does* not *eat* from faith; for whatever *is* not from faith is sin (Romans 14:23).

So the Lord said, "If you have faith as a mustard seed, you can say to this mulberry tree, 'Be pulled up by the roots and be planted in the sea,' and it would obey you" (Luke 17:6).

For in Christ Jesus neither circumcision nor un-circumcision avails anything, but faith working through love (Galatians 5:6).

Jesus said to her, "I am the resurrection and the life. He who believes in Me, though he may die, he shall live. And whoever lives and believes in Me shall never die. Do you believe this?" (John 11:25-26).

That He would grant you, according to the riches of His glory, to be strengthened with might through

His Spirit in the inner man, that Christ may dwell in your hearts through faith; that you, being rooted and grounded in love (Ephesians 3:16-17).

So *we are* always confident, knowing that while we are at home in the body we are absent from the Lord. For we walk by faith, not by sight (2 Corinthians 5:6-7).

"Most assuredly, I say to you, he who believes in Me has everlasting life" (John 6:47).

But Jesus turned around, and when He saw her He said, "Be of good cheer, daughter; your faith has made you well." And the woman was made well from that hour (Matthew 9:22).

Receive one who is weak in the faith, *but* not to disputes over doubtful things (Romans 14:1).

But you, O man of God, flee these things and pursue righteousness, godliness, faith, love, patience, gentleness (1 Timothy 6:11).

For with the heart one believes unto righteousness, and with the mouth confession is made unto salvation (Romans 10:10).

I tell you, no; but unless you repent you will all likewise perish (Luke 13:3).

Whom having not seen you love. Though now you do not see *Him,* yet believing, you rejoice with joy inexpressible and full of glory, [9] receiving the end of your faith—the salvation of *your* souls (1 Peter 1:8-9).

"Now the just shall live by faith; but if *anyone* draws back, My soul has no pleasure in him" (Hebrews 10:38).

And again He began to teach by the sea. And a great multitude was gathered to Him, so that He got into a boat and sat *in it* on the sea; and the whole multitude was on the land facing the sea. Then He taught them many things by parables, and said to them in His teaching… (Mark 4).

Commit your way to the LORD, trust also in Him, and He shall bring *it* to pass. He shall bring forth your righteousness as the light, and your justice as the noonday (Psalm 37:5-6).

"He who believes in Me, as the Scripture has said, out of his heart will flow rivers of living water" (John 7:38)

And my God shall supply all your need according to His riches in glory by Christ Jesus (Philippians 4:19).

For you are all sons of God through faith in Christ Jesus (Galatians 3:26).

But these are written that you may believe that Jesus is the Christ, the Son of God, and that believing you may have life in His name (John 20:31).

By faith Sarah herself also received strength to conceive seed, and she bore a child when she was past the age, because she judged Him faithful who had promised (Hebrews 11:11).

Having faith and a good conscience, which some having rejected, concerning the faith have suffered shipwreck (1 Timothy 1:19).

For we were saved in this hope, but hope that is seen is not hope; for why does one still hope for what he sees? But if we hope for what we do not see, we eagerly wait for *it* with perseverance (Romans 8:24-25).

Then Peter said to them, "Repent, and let every one of you be baptized in the name of Jesus Christ for the remission of sins; and you shall receive the gift of the Holy Spirit (Acts 2:38).

Then He said to the woman, "Your faith has saved you. Go in peace" (Luke 7:50).

Immediately the father of the child cried out and said with tears, "Lord, I believe; help my unbelief!" (Mark 9:24).

These things I have written to you who believe in the name of the Son of God, that you may know that you have eternal life, and that you may *continue to* believe in the name of the Son of God (1 John 5:13).

Therefore bear fruits worthy of repentance (Matthew 3:8).

For as many of you as were baptized into Christ have put on Christ (Galatians 3:27).

And he believed in the LORD, and He accounted it to him for righteousness (Genesis 15:6).

To one is given the word of wisdom through the Spirit, to another the word of knowledge through the same Spirit, to another faith by the same Spirit (1 Corinthians 12:8-9).

Then the Angel of the LORD called to Abraham a second time out of heaven, and said: "By Myself I have sworn, says the LORD, because you have done this thing, and have not withheld your son, your only *son*—blessing I will bless you, and multiplying I will multiply your descendants as the stars of the heaven and as the sand which *is* on the seashore; and your descendants shall possess the gate of their enemies. In your seed all the nations of the earth shall be blessed, because you have obeyed My voice" (Genesis 22:15-18).

Therefore know that the LORD your God, He *is* God, the faithful God who keeps covenant and mercy for a thousand generations with those who love Him and keep His commandments (Deuteronomy 7:9).

I would have lost heart, unless I had believed that I would see the goodness of the LORD in the land of the living. Wait on the LORD; be of good courage, and He shall strengthen your heart; wait, I say, on the LORD! (PSALM 27:13-14).

Though the fig tree may not blossom, nor fruit be on the vines; though the labor of the olive may fail, and the fields yield no food; though the flock may be cut off from the fold, and there be no herd in the stalls—yet I will rejoice in the LORD, I will joy in the God of my salvation. The LORD GOD IS MY STRENGTH; He will make my feet like deer's *feet,* and He will make me walk on my high hills (Habakkuk 3:17-19).

When Jesus heard *it,* He marveled, and said to

those who followed, "Assuredly, I say to you, I have not found such great faith, not even in Israel! And I say to you that many will come from east and west, and sit down with Abraham, Isaac, and Jacob in the kingdom of heaven. But the sons of the kingdom will be cast out into outer darkness. There will be weeping and gnashing of teeth." Then Jesus said to the centurion, "Go your way; and as you have believed, *so* let it be done for you." And his servant was healed that same hour (Matthew 8:10-13).

And when He had come into the house, the blind men came to Him. And Jesus said to them, "Do you believe that I am able to do this?" They said to Him, "Yes, Lord." Then He touched their eyes, saying, "According to your faith let it be to you" (Matthew 9:28-29).

When Jesus saw their faith, He said to the paralytic, "Son, your sins are forgiven you" (Mark 2:5).

And Stephen, full of faith and power, did great wonders and signs among the people (Acts 6:8).

Christ has redeemed us from the curse of the law, having become a curse for us (for it is written, "Cursed *is* everyone who hangs on a tree"), that the blessing of Abraham might come upon the Gentiles in Christ Jesus, that we might receive the promise of the Spirit through faith (Galatians 3:13-14).

There is one body and one Spirit, just as you were called in one hope of your calling; one Lord, one faith, one baptism; one God and Father of all, who *is* above all, and through all, and in you all (Ephesians 4:4-6).

Yet indeed I also count all things loss for the excellence of the knowledge of Christ Jesus my Lord, for whom I have suffered the loss of all things, and count them as rubbish, that I may gain Christ and be found in Him, not having my own righteousness, which *is* from the law, but that which *is* through faith in Christ, the righteousness which is from God by faith (Philippians 3:8-9).

An Invitation to Follow Jesus

Faith starts with a Person. His name is Jesus Christ. Jesus loves you so much and has a plan for your life. The Gospel reveals the plan that God has for you. God created us to be with Him, but it was our sin and our selfishness that separated us from God. Our sin cannot be removed by good works or by being a good person or even by paying for it. Jesus paid for our sins over two-thousand years ago by hanging on a bloody cross. He died, and He rose again so that all who put their faith in Him can have a new life. New life begins the moment you repent of your sins and put your faith in Christ Jesus. I believe that you can have a living faith today. I want to pray with you to make Jesus Christ the Lord of your life, and to allow His living faith into your heart, faith that will make you see from heaven's perspective. If you believe that Jesus is the Son of God, that He died and rose again, pray this with me right now.

Jesus, I need You. Forgive me of my sins. Forgive me of my selfishness. I don't want to be in charge anymore. Cleanse me with Your blood.

From this day forward, I'm putting my faith in You and not in myself. I want a living faith, not a dead faith. I receive You as my Savior, my Healer, and my Deliverer. And I renounce any other spirit that I've invited in my life, and I command it to leave me right now in Jesus' name. Holy Spirit fill me right now with Your presence and empower me to be a disciple of Jesus Christ who makes disciples who make disciples. Thank You, Jesus, that my faith in

You will cause me to have faith that sees from heaven's perspective.

If you just prayed that prayer and repented of your sins and made a choice to follow Jesus and be His disciple, I want to congratulate you, and so does all of heaven. There is a celebration for you right now. Below on this link, we have discipleship resources that we want to give to you for free. We pray the blessing of the Lord over your life, and that Jesus would lead and guide you into the new life that you have with Him.

www.compassiontoaction.com/newbeliever

Acknowledgments

When you find someone—or someone finds you—who sees from heaven's perspective and believes in you more than you believe in yourself, you have hit a gold mine, and your life becomes richer. I want to acknowledge some of my mentors and team members who have pulled the gold out of me and impacted me deeply.

Kris Vallotton, you saw and called something out in me in 1999 that helped shape the course of my life forever. You have been such a strength to me, and I will be forever grateful.

Bill Johnson, you taught me what it means to be an empowering leader and revealed the truth in the Gospel that I never really knew existed. And, that God not only uses those who stand behind a pulpit in a church, but He wants to use every believer in *power*.

Mark Brooks, you have been one of the most effective leaders and best friends in my life, not only a pastor and leader but also a friend who has been there for me in the lows and the highs. I tell everyone, wherever I go, that you are the best pastor in the world.

Lance Jacobs, I want to thank you for taking me under your wing when I was in ministry school. I wanted the Gospel to come out of me to touch the world around me. You created space for me and empowered me to lead while I was a student. I grew through your leadership, your belief in me, and through the opportunities you gave me. It altered the course of my life.

Danny Silk, you are a man of wisdom and insight. Thank you for challenging me in 2009 and encouraging me to grow personally. I look back now on our conversation in your office. It changed me. Thank you for believing in me even when my attitude was not the best. Thank you for reminding me of what God has called me to be and do. Your leadership has shaped my life.

Steve Backland, the summer I did an internship with you changed the course of my life. I would not be writing this book had you not told me in 2005 that I needed to learn how to use a computer because one day I would write books. Your belief in me and how you taught me to live by faith and not my feelings have not only impacted me, but also those who I have mentored. Steve, you are a leader of leaders, and I greatly admire your impact on my life and the lives of so many others.

Ricky Russ, Jr., thank you for your inspiration when it comes to writing. You helped make writing art for me and something that I enjoy, and you took the pressure off me that my style must be like others. Your influence on my life has greatly impacted my creativity.

Lastly, I want to thank my Compassion To Action team who have stood with me and made me a better leader. I want to give a special thank you to Fay Dennis who has helped me write this book and who has started to help me write others. Fay, your servant's heart and work ethic have impacted me greatly. Thank you for all the hard work you have put into this book and others. It is a win for you and me as many read this book and are impacted to see through faith that leads to action. A big thank you once again.

Connect With Us

www.compassiontoaction.com

Facebook: @compassiontoactionofficial

Facebook: @chris.overstreet.37

Instagram: @compassion_to_action

YouTube: Chris Overstreet - Compassion To Action

Made in the USA
Lexington, KY
20 December 2019